LEVEL 1

YOU READ | I READ

City and Country

Jody Jensen Shaffer

NATIONAL GEOGRAPHIC

Washington, D.C.

How to Use This Book

Reading together is fun! When older and younger readers share the experience, it opens the door to new learning. As you read together, talk about what you learn.

YOU READ

This side is for a parent, older sibling, or older friend. Before reading each page, take a look at the words and pictures. Talk about what you see. Point out words that might be hard for the younger reader.

I READ

This side is for the younger reader.

As you read, look for the bolded words. Talk about them before you read. In each chapter, the bolded words are: Chapter 1: describing city and country • Chapter 2: describing words • Chapter 3: sense words • Chapter 4: action words

At the end of each chapter, do the activity together.

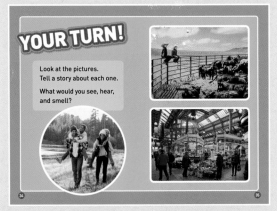

Table of Contents

Places Around the World

 YOU READ

Look out your window!
Do you see buildings,
traffic, and crowded streets?
If so, you live in a city.
A city is an **urban** area.

4

I READ

Every city is different. An **urban** area is a place where many people live and work.

5

YOU READ

Maybe you look outside and see lots of open space. If so, you live in the country. The country is **rural.** Rural is the opposite of urban.

6

A **rural** area can have fields and farms. It can have mountains, too.

7

YOUR TURN!

Look at the pictures.
Do they show a place that
is urban or rural?

How do you know?

A

B

C

D

ANSWERS: A. rural; B. urban; C. rural; D. urban

9

CHAPTER 2

City Home, Country Home

 YOU READ

No matter where you live,
there's no place like home.
Many people in the world live in
big cities. Cities are full of people.

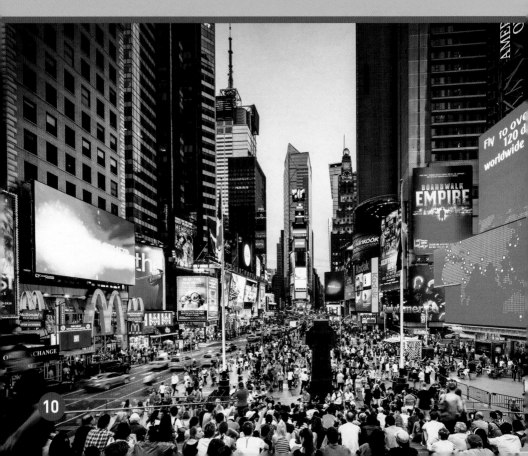

10

 In **big** cities, homes are close together. Lots of people share the same outdoor space.

YOU READ

In the country, there is more space and **fewer** people. There is a lot of space to run and play outside.

Homes are often far apart. People have **fewer** neighbors.

13

YOU READ

Many people in the city live in row homes. Row homes share at least one wall with another home. Row homes sometimes look **alike.**

14

In the country, homes don't touch each other. They don't always look **alike.**

15

 YOU READ

In the city, people also live in apartments. **Tall** apartment buildings have many levels inside. There are lots of homes on each level, and people can ride the elevator up and down!

16

In the country, most homes have fewer levels. Houses aren't as **tall.** They have more space to be wide.

17

YOU READ

City people don't always have much green space. They find creative ways to share the land, though. They grow **pretty** flowers and vegetables together.

 In the country, many people have big yards. They can grow their own **pretty** flowers and vegetables.

19

YOUR TURN!

Match the picture to the word. Draw a line with your finger.

Word Bank

row house

yard

apartment

house

CHAPTER 3
Sights and Sounds

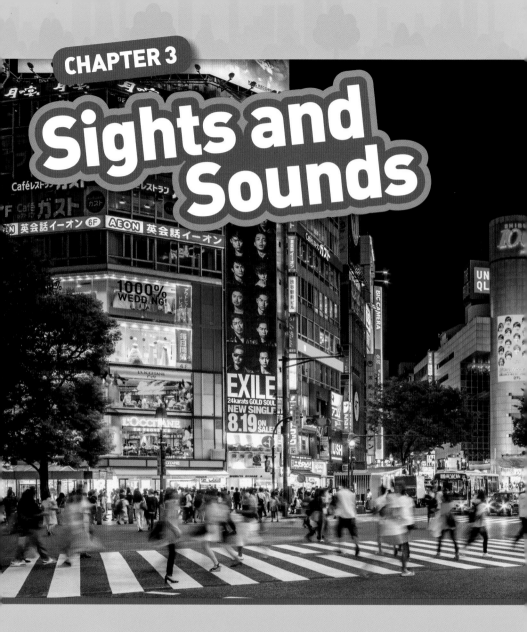

 There are lots of things to **see** in the city. Tall buildings tower over people and traffic. Bright lights blink. People are all around.

22

You can **see** people traveling in the city. They take trains, buses, and taxis.

23

YOU READ

In the country, you might **see** rolling green fields. Goats, cows, and sheep roam through pastures. They eat the grass in the countryside.

24

You can **see** lakes in the country. People play and swim in the water.

 Cities are full of sounds. You can **hear** street musicians singing, kids playing in the park, and friends laughing in crowded shops.

26

In the city, you can **hear** taxis honk. Street sellers call out loudly.

27

YOU READ

Sounds fill the country, too. You can **hear** cows mooing and trains whistling. Tractors rumble across fields, and insects chirp day and night.

 In the country, you can **hear** water rushing in a stream. Frogs croak and fish splash.

29

 YOU READ

There are lots of things to **smell** in the city. People sell spicy vegetables on the sidewalk. The smell of freshly baked bread fills the air outside a corner bakery.

 You can **smell** many different things when people live close together.

YOU READ

In the country, you can **smell** freshly cut grass. The air is clean, and the smells of nature are all around.

32

Some people live near cornfields. They **smell** sweet corn when it gets picked. You can see, hear, and smell things everywhere!

33

YOUR TURN!

Look at the pictures.
Tell a story about each one.

What would you see, hear, and smell?

CHAPTER 4

Life in the City and the Country

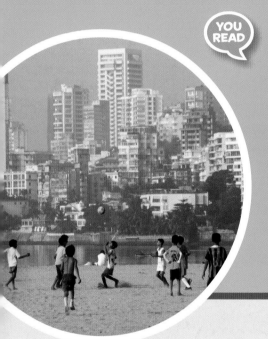

YOU READ

No matter where they live, people in the city and in the country like to do many of the same things. They play sports. They ride bikes. They work and **go** to school.

36

 Both city people and country people visit museums and **go** to concerts.

37

YOU READ

Some city people take walks for fun. People **walk** on trails that wind through city parks.

 In the country, some people **walk** in the woods. They hike up and down mountain trails.

YOU READ

Some city people take taxis and subways to get around. They might walk or bike to work and school. Sometimes people **ride** city buses to travel longer distances.

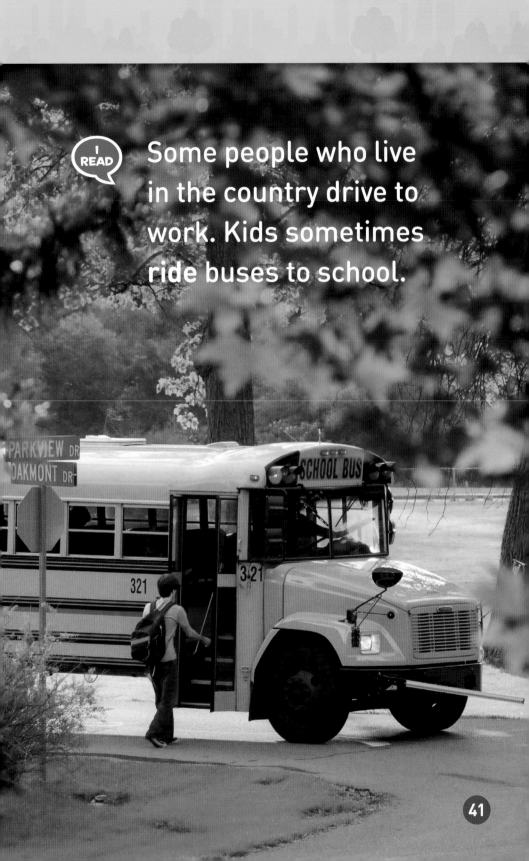

I READ Some people who live in the country drive to work. Kids sometimes **ride** buses to school.

YOU READ

Students in city and country schools **learn** about similar things. Children everywhere study math, science, and history. They might take art and music classes, too.

42

Many students **learn** about sports at school. Kids in the city and country like to run and play!

43

YOU READ

Wherever people live, they call it home. People who live in the city **like** to learn, play, and work. People who live in the country do, too.

44

I READ Everyone **likes** to be with family and friends. No matter where home is, there is no place like it!

45

YOUR TURN!

What is it like where you live? What do you like to do?

For Tom, Madeline, and Sam. My home is where you are. —J. J. S.

Copyright © 2017 National Geographic Partners, LLC

Published by National Geographic Partners, LLC, Washington, D.C. 20036. All rights reserved. Reproduction in whole or in part without written permission of the publisher is prohibited.

NATIONAL GEOGRAPHIC and Yellow Border Design are trademarks of the National Geographic Society, used under license.

The author and publisher gratefully acknowledge the expert literacy review of this book by Kimberly Gillow, Principal, Milan Area Schools, Michigan.

Author's Note: There are many kinds of urban and rural areas around the world. There are also many similarities. There are many differences. As you read, think and talk about the different kinds of urban, suburban, and rural areas you know about.

Library of Congress Cataloging-in-Publication Data
Names: Shaffer, Jody Jensen, author.
Title: City and country / Jody Jensen Shaffer.
Description: Washington, D.C. : National Geographic, 2017. | Series: National Geographic readers | Audience: Age 2 to 5. | Audience: Pre-school. | Identifiers: LCCN 2016051351 (print) | LCCN 2017017328 (ebook) | ISBN 9781426328886 (e-book) | ISBN 9781426328862 (paperback) | ISBN 9781426328879 (hardcover)
Subjects: LCSH: City and town life--Juvenile literature | Country life--Juvenile literature. | BISAC: JUVENILE NONFICTION / Readers /Beginner.
Classification: LCC HT152 (ebook) | LCC HT152 .S53 2017 (print) | DDC 307.76--dc23
LC record available at https://lccn.loc.gov/2016051351

National Geographic supports K–12 educators with ELA Common Core Resources. Visit natgeoed.org/commoncore for more information.

Printed in the United States of America
17/WOR/1